Resea

Research Without Tears

From the First Ideas to Published Output

John Creedy

The Truby Williams Professor of Economics, University of Melbourne, Australia

Edward Elgar

Cheltenham, UK • Northampton, MA, USA

Published by
Edward Elgar Publishing Limited
Glensanda House
Montpellier Parade
Cheltenham
Glos GL50 1UA
UK

Edward Elgar Publishing, Inc.
William Pratt House
9 Dewey Court
Northampton
Massachusetts 01060
USA

A catalogue record for this book
is available from the British Library

Library of Congress Control Number: 2007047865

ISBN 978 1 84720 814 9 (cased)
ISBN 978 1 84720 834 7 (paperback)

Printed and bound in Great Britain by MPG Books Ltd,
Bodmin, Cornwall

Contents

Preface

This book arose from a series of talks, given over a number of years, on starting a research project, writing research papers and publishing. These talks in turn stemmed from the view that all researchers can benefit from thinking explicitly about the many facets of the research experience, rather than carrying out the tasks in an unconscious manner and learning, with luck, from experience. Some things can only be fully appreciated following experience, but I believe that life is too short to learn everything from experience, and anyway the costs can often be severe and indeed distressing. A little advice can therefore go a long way. While there is no doubt that research is difficult, it does not have to be accompanied by anxieties and distress.

It seems to be inevitable that many of the most important lessons can sound, when stated plainly to people who have not yet gained any experience, platitudinous. Anyone who gives advice frequently has to listen, some time later, to people quoting their earlier instructions and lessons as if they were wonderful and original insights. The most frequently quoted example in the present context is the truth that everything takes longer than you think. The only sensible response is to agree. To give up any attempt to communicate those lessons does not seem to be the responsible attitude. But with this in mind, I would urge the reader to re-read various sections of this book at intervals during their first research and writing efforts. It will at least reassure them that they are not alone in their new-found experience.

Discussions with other researchers quickly reveal that the variety of experiences, in relation to research, writing, supervision, university procedures and regula-tions, is huge. Students also differ considerably in their aptitude, character and approach to work. In giving advice, different people therefore have different priorities and preoccupations. So it is inevitable that people prefer to attach different stresses and priorities from those I have given below. I can only state that there are few absolute rules and that the recommendations given in this book are based on my own experience of research and of supervising numerous students.

This book owes much to my earlier papers in Greedy (2001, 2006, 2007), though these have been revised substantially. particularly the first paper. I have benefited from numerous comments and encourage-ment, for which I am most grateful, from Siobhan Austen, Harry Bloch, Jeff Borland, Sheila Cameron, Mark Casson, Iris Claus, Robert Dixon, Edward Elgar, Nisvan Erkal, John Fender, Norman Gemmell, Dominique Gross, Ross Guest, Veronica Jacobsen, Guyonne Kalb, Tim Kam, Stuart Kells, Anke Leroux, Ingrid

Linsley, Joanne Loundes, Solmaz Moslehi, Denis O'Brien, Derek Ritzmann and Justin van de Ven.

I have been particularly fortunate in having received highly valued advice over the years, and I have been privileged to be able closely to observe exemplary scholars at work. I should like to take this opportunity yet again to pay tribute to just two people who gave invaluable advice and support to me at early stages in my career. First, J.A.C. (Alan) Brown, as my own supervisor, was a tremendous inspiration in so many ways. Second, P.E. (Peter) Hart gave considerable support, with crucial advice, and provided a superb role model during my early career as a lecturer. If this book succeeds in helping any new researchers, much is owed to these two outstanding people.

Part I

Introduction

Chapter 1

Introduction and Outline

The aim of this book is to provide a brief guide for those starting their first research project and writing a paper, report or thesis. The process of planning and executing a research project, and producing a research paper which communicates results in a clear and succinct way, is far from self-evident even to those with extensive experience of writing other types of report or essay. This book therefore sets down explicitly some of those things which even experienced researchers often take for granted.

The first anxiety facing new researchers concerns the problem of how to start, as research is so different from any other kind of activity involved in coursework. The primary requirement is to formulate a well-defined question. A statement or description of a topic or area of research interest is merely the first stage in the important process of arriving at a clear focus. You cannot really be considered as having a research topic until it can be expressed in the form of a succinct question. Chapter 2 therefore concentrates on how to get started and discusses the special nature of research.

When thinking about the qualities required to complete a research project, it is useful to keep in mind the three 'Cs' of research: these are curiosity, concentration and confidence. Curiosity is the major stimulus to research, and as Dorothy Parker famously said, 'The cure for boredom is curiosity. There is no cure for curiosity.' Intense concentration is needed to solve the difficulties that inevitably lie along the research path. Confidence – mixed with a good dose of courage – is needed to sustain the effort.

In writing a research paper, the major objective, which cannot be overstated, is the achievement of clarity. What is needed is a transparent statement of the question examined, the methods used and results. This is much more difficult than is usually realised. A willingness to respond to constructive criticisms and suggestions, along with requests for clarification, is essential. It is necessary to develop an appropriate style of writing, one that is quite different from styles used for other purposes. Chapter 3 provides some practical suggestions for organising the writing of a research paper and giving it the appropriate 'shape' or appearance: it must look like a serious piece of research. These suggestions should of course also be supplemented by careful study of the writing styles of favourite and exemplary authors.

After discussing the production of a first research paper, some suggestions regarding study for a PhD are made. For many people their first research project marks the beginning of work on a doctoral thesis. The emphasis in chapter 4 is on aspects which are particularly relevant when doing the kind of large scale and substantial work involved in a PhD thesis. The role of a supervisor is also extremely important and this is also discussed. It is valuable to think explicitly about the processes involved in doing this work, rather than stumbling from stage to stage in an unconscious manner. It is clear that PhD experiences vary widely among students, just as the needs and characters of students and their supervisors vary. Inevitably the suggestions made here reflect my own personal views involving subjective judgements based on experience as a supervisor.

The advice is primarily directed towards students, though some academics who are new to supervising may also find some helpful suggestions. The chapter is addressed largely to relatively young full-time students who are doing a PhD soon after completing undergraduate studies – the majority of graduate students. Those who are part-time PhD students face particular additional challenges, not discussed here. The advice is perhaps more relevant for theses completed in Australian and UK universities, compared with US universities, where coursework plays a more significant role and the thesis often consists of just three chapters on separate topics, rather than containing a more sustained treatment of one field of research. Furthermore, the role of the supervisor differs among countries. However, there are obviously many common features.

The path from manuscript to publication, either in journal or book form, is then examined. It is perhaps tempting to believe that the hard work involved in producing research ends with the completion of a manuscript. In reality, the path from manuscript to publication can present many hazards not met during the research itself, and involves a new and quite different type of learning process. The various stages of the publication process are designed to act as a selection device, or filter, and to improve the quality of the final product itself. Without these features it is likely that many more articles and books would contain serious errors or material that is unclear or directed to a narrower audience than necessary. Of course, where subjective judgements are involved concerning the value of work, it is possible that the same filter prevents some useful material from being published, or being published in the most appropriate form.

Chapter 5 indicates some of the main features of the publication process, so that readers may be in a better position to make judgements about published work and writers may be, to some extent at least, prepared to face the difficulties that inevitably lie in their path. Chapter 6 concentrates on the complex process involved in publishing papers in refereed journals.

While some of the features of research and publishing are common to all disciplines, there are important differences. This book is necessarily written with economists in mind, although it is hoped that other researchers may find it helpful.

Part II

A First Research Paper

Chapter 2

Starting Research

This chapter provides advice for those undertaking their first research project. The process of planning and executing a research project, and producing a research paper which communicates results in a clear and succinct way, is far from self-evident even to those with extensive experience of writing other types of report or essay. Research goes through a number of stages, discussed below, and it is useful to think about the process in terms of the metaphor of climbing a mountain. Thus it is best to take just one step at a time, with a clear focus on the path, rather than rushing ahead recklessly or being daunted by the distant peak high in the mist. However, at regular intervals it is good to stop to look around and take in the view. One's perspective on the research changes on looking back from the peak. Special insights are obtained: the famous economist Edgeworth referred to special alpine flowers found in their rarefied atmosphere. However, there is a danger of forgetting just how difficult the journey has been and how much has been learned along the route. The path to the peak may have been uncomfortable in places and was unlikely to have been the most direct route. But in subsequently guiding other people to the top of the mountain, it is important to avoid taking them along all the detours and dead ends. As a guide, you should highlight the best views and take the most comfortable route.

The nature of the research process is described in section 2.1. This is necessary because research is so different from other forms of activity. In arriving at a research topic and formulating a plan, it is usually necessary to transform and narrow a broad topic by a process of improving the focus, so that it deals with a well-defined and interesting problem that can be handled within an appropriate time period. Suggestions for arriving at a precise research topic and making a start on research are made in section 2.2. This section also stresses the importance of careful planning, even though many problems and contingencies cannot be foreseen.

2.1 The Nature of Research

In popular language, the word 'research' seems to have become associated simply with any process of gathering existing information. However, research is a process of making new discoveries. These discoveries may include new empirical regularities, new theoretical results or improved understanding of and fresh insights into a problem. The research paper needs to say something quite new, rather than collating or rehearsing existing knowledge. Sometimes research projects may lead to 'negative' results. For example, these might include the finding that an econometric model, which previously provided a good fit to observed data, no longer performs well or does not apply to another country. While researchers prefer to obtain new 'positive' results, such negative results are useful and should not be dismissed.

The desire to say something new presents a difficult challenge. Contrary to a popular illusion, progress in research is largely achieved by making a series of small steps, rather than taking giant leaps.

A distinguishing feature of research is that it is usually the researcher who formulates the precise question to be examined and decides on the approach used. Indeed, the precise specification of the problem examined is an important element in planning a project. It should be possible to describe the research project in terms of a clear question. The question has to be clearly defined and seen to be worthy of attention. Any research project needs to be well motivated. Other people cannot automatically be assumed to find your research interesting or important.

The need to say something new necessarily involves a movement into unknown territory. There is no easy way to know if the answers are right or if the best method of attack is being followed. All researchers face a series of hurdles which must be overcome and there is seldom a 'correct' approach but instead a range of potential alternatives. Research therefore involves not only the continual exercise of judgement, but also a degree of confidence and willingness to take risks. In addition, there is no way to avoid occasionally following false leads and reaching an impasse, that is, going down 'dead ends'. By their very nature, the reasons for particular judgements are not obvious to other people, so it is necessary to convince readers of the paper that the various steps and assumptions made are sensible; such acceptance cannot be taken for granted.

These aspects combine to ensure that research is interesting and intellectually rewarding, while it also gives rise to alternating phases of optimism and pessimism. There are times when all researchers feel overwhelmed by difficulties, and are confused, anxious and not at all sure that they have anything worth reporting. At other times progress can seem unusually rapid, often helped by what can only be described as the substantial role played by serendipity, where happy discoveries are made by accident. However, these happy accidents usually only arise after much concentrated thought on the topic; in other words, 'fortune favours the prepared mind'.

Experienced researchers know that they will go through these alternating phases and that they can 'work through' them. For those who are carrying out research for the first time, it is worth anticipating these features and understanding that such experience is not unique.

2.1.1 The Nonlinear Nature of Research

A simplistic view of research may be described in terms of a linear model in which the first stage involves reading as much as possible on a chosen topic and, after having a brilliant idea of how to proceed, this is followed by the analysis. The process is completed by simply writing down the results in a coherent and readable form that will instantly establish the author's world-wide fame. However, nothing could be further from the truth. Progress in research is actually highly nonlinear. It involves a complex process described in terms of a repeated cycle of writing and returning to further analyses and reading. Furthermore, papers are often completed as a result of the pressure of deadlines, or the need to turn to other work, rather than ending in a dramatic flourish.

Writing is itself a process of discovery, not least of the author's own level of understanding. It reveals gaps in the argument and suggests new avenues of research as well as, importantly, providing an error-trapping process. Most good research, however narrowly defined it may initially appear, has its own momentum. That is, the process of researching a particular topic leads to further questions and issues for investigation. The completion of a research paper is therefore often accompanied by negative feelings that, after all, not much has been achieved. It is worth remembering that this is simply an aspect of the general truth that the more we learn, the more conscious we are of our ignorance. When worrying that you have not really made any progress, it is worth thinking back to the initial stages of the project – it will soon become clear just how far you have moved forward. Results and approaches are often only 'obvious' with the benefit of hindsight.

2.1.2 The Ingredients of Research

There is one fundamental ingredient without which research can never begin: that ingredient is curiosity. In addition to curiosity, research also requires a willingness and the energy to pursue various avenues, even if some of these may lead to a dead end. Furthermore, research needs imagination and flexibility to overcome the many inevitable problems along the road. Research also requires good judgement in selecting the appropriate techniques of analysis, deciding which aspects can be safely ignored and which assumptions are fundamental for the particular context, and assessing the value of the results at each stage. The best research reports will reflect these qualities.

Research also involves intense concentration over long periods. It is not possible to return to a research project casually at irregular intervals or only when there are no other pressing commitments. It is necessary to allocate regular times to research and to keep a project moving forward. Indeed, concentration has to be such that research becomes something that is extremely hard to *stop* thinking about. When this stage is reached it is quite common for researchers to wake in the morning with the solution to a problem that seemed intractable before going to sleep.

It is worth keeping in mind the following 'rules' regarding the role of time in research. These rules provide a further example of the fact that some of the most important truths appear at first sight to be highly platitudinous, and much experience is often required before their importance is fully appreciated.

1. There is no simple relationship between inputs of time and outputs of useful results. All research meets difficulties. Overcoming them may take a few minutes or it may take days or weeks. Successful research requires a willingness to do whatever is needed in order to overcome the problem.[1]

2. Virtually everything takes longer than is anticipated, often considerably longer. The problem is compounded by the fact that things take longer than we think – even when we know that they take longer than we think. Eventually every researcher comes to appreciate the importance of this lesson after painful experience.

2.2 Getting Started

Some researchers may be faced with a broad research question that other people have suggested, or that arises from a practical policy issue. Their main initial problem is to

[1] This has of course to be qualified by the point that eventually it may be realised that a dead end has been reached.

decide on the research plan, involving the method of attack. It is nearly always necessary to refine the statement of the problem, in particular to narrow the scope of the project further so that it is more clearly defined and manageable. As part of this process it is extremely important to express the topic in the form of an explicit question; if this cannot be done, it is likely that the subject is not well defined. The initial temptation, to be strongly resisted, is to raise 'big' questions which would occupy a lifetime of research.

In clarifying the research plan, much benefit can often be gained from discussions with other people, particularly experienced researchers who are familiar with the area and its potential problems. Think in terms of taking a number of small steps, rather than making great strides.

Many people who are new to research believe that a search of the relevant literature is part of the project. But it is more appropriate to view an initial investigation of the literature as a necessary preliminary exercise, so that it is part of the planning stage. Indeed, a research project cannot be properly planned without an understanding of what other people have achieved, what methods and data (where appropriate) are needed, and what difficulties are likely to be faced.

It is too often assumed that the data required to carry out an empirical investigation are available, especially if it is planned to replicate another study for a different country. The collection and examination of data should also be regarded as a necessary part of the planning of a project. It usually comes as a surprise to new researchers to learn just how difficult it normally is to obtain necessary data. Often proxies or approximations are needed. When the data have been collected, it is useful to carry out preliminary exercises to assess their reliability. Many projects have foundered because of over-optimism regarding data.

Experienced researchers may often be able to take a specific question, sometimes arising from their earlier work, and begin working on it by taking an independent approach. For example, they can effectively sit down with a blank piece of paper and begin to construct an appropriate model. Further, a quality of good research is that it has its own 'momentum'. But those who are new to research usually need explicitly to link their work more closely to existing literature. Hence first research projects usually proceed by making modifications to and extensions of earlier work.

The process of investigating the literature has been considerably eased by the existence of computer search facilities. But great care needs to be taken in using these aids. Only a familiarity with the subject can provide an indication of the 'keywords' that are likely to be fruitful. Some bibliographic databases are limited to journals, and necessarily only a selection of these are included, so that important contributions in books may be overlooked.

There is no alternative to getting one's hands dirty in a library. Examine the relevant specialist and general journals. Importantly, follow up the references given in the articles to other work which appears relevant. You will gradually learn who are the major contributors to a particular area, the special vocabulary or argot used, and the best places to look for further information.

2.2.1 Clarifying the Research Question

The following suggestions are designed to make the process of arriving at a precise research question or approach reasonably systematic. When reading journal articles or other research papers, keep the following points in mind.

1. Journal papers are usually terse. They represent work which has matured over several years and editors nearly always ask for papers to be reduced in length before publication. Hence, a full understanding of the methods and the significance of the results can only be obtained after detailed and extensive study, involving re-reading journal articles several times. Investigate whether an earlier version, in the form of a Discussion or Working Paper, is available. This can often provide more details.

2. However, a quick initial read is generally enough to allow identification of the main question considered by the author, the methods of analysis used, the data required and the nature of the results. These are the four major features that should receive your initial attention.

3. After this preliminary look at particular papers, it is

possible to judge whether they are of potential interest. You may reject several papers in this way before finding one that stimulates you to look closer. If you continue studying the paper, make notes about other literature cited in it, data used, analytical methods and principal results.

4. Even at this early stage, keep orderly notes about the works consulted, including full bibliographical details. It can be extremely time consuming at a later stage to have to go back to the library to obtain simple details like volume and page numbers.

The importance of curiosity has already been mentioned. Constantly asking questions must become a research habit. When reading papers, it is important always to ask questions, such as:

1. Can the approach used in a study be applied to other contexts, countries or time periods?

2. What assumptions are implicit? Are all the assumptions sensible? To what extent might the results be sensitive to the assumptions? How can they be relaxed? Are there any unnecessary assumptions? To criticise a paper on the grounds that it makes a number of assumptions is beside the point, as all research requires assumptions. The skill is in avoiding 'throwing the baby out with the bath water'. This refers to the need to make assumptions which allow simplifications and

concentration on the problem at hand, while not making it trivial.

3. Is the approach used the appropriate one? Have new techniques been developed since the paper was first written?

4. Have all relevant statistical tests been carried out? Are the results consistent with expectations, or with earlier work?

5. Precise data relating to the theoretical concepts are often not available. Are the surrogate or constructed variables the most appropriate for the task? If a relevant variable has been omitted, can anything be said about the likely bias?

6. Are there any implications of the study which have not been fully drawn out by the author? Can these be exploited in your work?

The most important question to ask, the one which actually gets the research underway, is the one which begins with the words 'what if ...?', such as 'what if I use a different specification ...?', or 'what if I drop a particular condition ...?', and so on.

2.2.2 The Plan of Attack

Research should not be allowed to drift along in a haphazard way. Do not allow it to lapse as it is very hard indeed to pick up research after an interval – a large 'fixed cost' is involved in becoming familiar again with all the important components. Planning is crucial, even though there are nearly always unanticipated difficulties which cause the plan to be revised. It is useful to have a plan for the 'big picture' as well as having daily or weekly lists of things to be done. Establish good work habits to make efficient use of your time. For example, there may be a short 'gap' in the day where you have no other commitments. Good use can be made of the short interval by fitting in a specific task such as working on the bibliography or a short section, or producing and tidying diagrams and tables. Each morning, think about what you are going to do before arriving at your desk.

1. Attach a time schedule to the plan. When working to a deadline, aim to finish with several weeks to spare. This will allow time to leave the paper alone for a while and then give it a final polish after returning to it with fresh eyes. It is surprising how many small but significant improvements can be made in this final stage.

2. Start writing immediately. As mentioned above, writing is itself a process of discovery, revealing gaps in the argument (and your own understanding) and suggesting new lines of enquiry.

2.3 Conclusions

There is no easy formula for producing good research papers. Research requires curiosity, energy, imagination and flexibility to overcome the inevitable problems. It also requires good judgement to select the appropriate assumptions and techniques of analysis, and to assess the value of results. The best research reflects these qualities.

Many challenges must be overcome and even researchers with considerable experience cannot avoid going down dead ends. All work must be checked as carefully as possible.

All this takes longer than envisaged. When planning research projects, produce a generous estimate, fully allowing for the fact that everything takes longer – then double the time and add some more for good measure. This is not an exaggeration.

This chapter has described the special nature of research and the ways in which it differs from other work. It has provided some suggestions regarding ways to get started in formulating a research proposal. In defining a research topic, the ability to state a clear question is important, rather than simply describing a broad topic. A useful imaginary test of whether you have a clear question giving a focus for your research is the 'elevator test'. Imagine that you enter an elevator to travel just a few floors, and someone who is not a specialist in your subject asks you what your research is about. Within the short space of time before the doors open again and your questioner moves away, you need to be able to communicate your research aims.

Research may be said to involve three 'Cs'. First, a necessary requirement is curiosity. Second, the ability to bring a research project to completion requires intense concentration. Third, the willingness to take a 'leap in the dark' and overcome difficult problems requires a degree of confidence, tempered with a realistic attitude. The experience of a first successful research project should provide a boost to confidence when further difficulties are inevitably encountered.

Chapter 3

Writing a Research Paper

The previous chapter ended by referring to the three 'Cs' of research – curiosity, concentration and confidence. In writing a research report or paper, it may be said that there are also three 'Cs' – clarity, clarity and clarity. This major objective – the achievement of clarity – cannot be overstated. Hence, avoid using metaphors, vague allusions, cryptic comments or rhetorical flourishes.

What is needed is a transparent statement of the issues, methods and results. This is much more difficult than is usually realised. A willingness to respond to constructive criticisms and suggestions, along with requests for clarification, is essential. It is necessary to develop an appropriate style of writing, one that is quite different from that used for other purposes. It is best to recognise at the outset that the writing process is not easy. Think explicitly about the challenge and style to be adopted, rather than launching into the task unconsciously. Here it is worth recalling the advice of Samuel Johnson that, 'what is written without effort is in general read without pleasure'. All this does not mean that the writing process cannot be a pleasant and highly satisfying task.

This chapter provides some brief practical suggestions for organising the writing of a research paper and giving it the appropriate 'shape' or appearance so that it 'looks right'. The typical structure, or shape, of a research paper is described in section 3.1. Special attention is given to the introduction, the review of previous literature and conclusions, as these features present special problems. A research paper must satisfy certain fundamental scholarly requirements or proprieties; these are also explained. Section 3.2 provides some suggestions regarding the basic layout and appearance of the report. This concerns such things as the use of tables, footnotes and citations.

Some suggestions regarding the writing process are given in section 3.3, which includes recommendations regarding features to avoid. Section 3.4 provides some checklists. No attempt is made here to provide advice regarding grammar or sentence construction, or other details. A range of guides exist for this purpose. On report writing see, for example, Taylor (1989), Anderson and Poole (1994), Evans and Gruba (2002) and Neugeboren (2005). On English usage see, for example, Cutts (1995), Weiner (1995), Seely (1998), Allen (1999) and Law (2001).

3.1 The Structure of a Research Paper

A research paper must have the following characteristics.

1. It should demonstrate a clear perception of the research problem, its relation to the 'bigger picture' and the relevant literature.

2. It should provide motivation for the research question and the support for the approach used.

3. It should provide a clear statement of the methods used and the major results. A paper should demonstrate an ability to formulate a useful approach and provide support for judgements made in selecting techniques and data.

4. It must show an appreciation of the value and limitations of the results.

To achieve these ends, a research paper must be given a clear structure, which is helpful to the writer and the reader. The development of the argument needs to be transparent, so that the reader knows how any particular part of the paper fits into the whole. The following advice to theatrical producers, by W.S. Gilbert, may appear to be rather broad, but is worth repeating in this context: 'Tell 'em what you are going to do; let 'em see you doing it; then tell 'em what you have done.'

Although metaphors are really best avoided when writing research papers, conducting research has been described in terms of climbing a mountain. Here a similar metaphor applies of taking the reader of a research paper on a journey. The reader needs to have confidence in you as a guide. It is not reasonable simply to say 'follow closely behind me'. People feel much more comfortable when they are given information about what to expect on the route ahead and where the particular path, though it may not obviously seem to be the best to take, is likely to lead. Furthermore, the speed of travelling needs to be varied. There must be rests where followers are allowed to pause and enjoy the view, and perhaps be reminded of some aspects of the next part of the route ahead.

A clear development is achieved by dividing the paper into sections, within which there may be subsections, and possibly subsubsections. However, the vast majority of papers need only three levels of headings; these are the main title, section and subsection headings. The titles should be brief and informative, and the first sentence after a title or subtitle should not rely on the title for its meaning. It should therefore not begin with the words, 'This is ...', which assumes that the reader knows to what 'this' refers. Ensure that there are appropriate linkages between the various sections, to ensure continuity. These links help to clarify the logical structure of the paper. The use of titles is discussed further, along with other features of the layout of a paper, in section 3.2 below.

The first section is of course the introduction, and a typical structure involves subsequent sections describing the development of a framework or model, the description of data and techniques used (where appropriate), theoretical or empirical results, further developments possibly including policy analyses, and finally a concluding section. The introduction may briefly discuss previous literature, or may be followed by a separate section providing a literature review. The introduction and literature review are much harder to write than is often assumed, and are therefore discussed in more detail here.

3.1.1 The Introduction

The introduction is a crucial part of the paper; it often determines whether the reader continues or discards the paper. Even experienced researchers expect to have to revise their introductions many times, often substantially. In particular, it is worth returning to your introduction at the last stage in the 'polishing' process, as your understanding of the precise contribution made by the paper improves. As suggested by Blaise Pascal, 'the last thing one knows in constructing a work is what to put in first'. But do not leave its writing until the end. The first attempt to write the introduction helps to sort out your own views and priorities. Writing an introduction is often a matter of finding the right 'key' to open up the paper. It is then easier to write the later sections.

An introduction needs to let the reader know, as quickly as possible, three important things. It must answer the questions 'what is the research question to be examined in the paper?', 'why is it worth studying?' and 'how is it going to be tackled?'. Therefore, it is useful to think in terms of providing the 'what, why and how' of the paper. The reader needs to understand these features before being willing to devote time and patience to the rest of the argument.

Do not digress, or fall into the trap of writing 'content free' sentences in an overlong preamble. A common content-free opening sentence informs the reader that, ' .... has been the subject of considerable debate in recent years'. State the specific question examined in the paper as directly and quickly as possible. One journal editor has suggested that in the vast majority of papers submitted to the journal, it is possible to omit the first paragraph without loss. There is much truth in this comment – many writers seem reluctant to start without some kind of preamble which typically serves no useful purpose.

Do not be tempted to add material that should rightfully be placed in the concluding section. Say what is already known and signal what is new about your own paper, without making extravagant or empty claims or being negative about previous work. For example, avoid the all-too-common sentence along the lines of, 'To the best of the author's knowledge, this paper is the first to add an extra year of data to previous studies.'

The introduction therefore provides, as well as a statement of aims, the motivation for the study and the particular approach adopted. However, remember that the introduction should be intelligible to someone turning to the topic for the first time. The paper may be read in the future by people who are not immersed in current debates and terms. It should not be addressed to the few specialists who are completely familiar with the area, so do not be allusive.

An important role of the introduction is to give the reader a clear view of the structure of the paper, so some kind of outline is needed. Provide plenty of signposts to point the way forward. These can most easily be added at a later stage, after the first draft has been completed.

3.1.2 The Literature Review

The aim of a literature review is to place your own work clearly within its larger context. While research involves a focus on a narrow range of questions, it is obviously important to understand how it relates to wider issues. A brief review of the existing literature can help to provide some motivation for your own analysis. In addition, it is only possible to establish a claim to have extended the literature by making clear the relevant contributions of others. However, bear in mind that it may often be better to discuss earlier literature in the course of setting out your own analysis. References to the literature can then be made in support of your approach, or in order to contrast or compare results. This can often be achieved relatively quickly.

Sometimes it may be necessary to provide an extensive review of earlier literature. This presents a difficult challenge as it calls for a mature and confident approach resulting from long familiarity with the problem. For this reason, the literature review is often the weakest part of the work of people who are relatively new to research. Ideally, the discussion of the literature should be organised along analytical or taxonomic lines. This form of arrangement provides clear criteria for deciding whether, and where, an earlier work needs to be mentioned.

In writing a review, keep the following suggestions in mind.

1. Start with a clear statement of the broad problem.

2. Distinguish alternative possible approaches, whose features may be analytical, involving a range of assumptions and techniques, or statistical/econometric, associated with data constraints and estimation techniques.

3. Refer to earlier contributions in the context of these different approaches. Some works may therefore be included only as part of a list while others, judged to be the most important, may require further discussion.

4. Indicate the strengths and weaknesses, in your judgement and without being unduly negative, of the various approaches and explain precisely where your study fits into the taxonomy or framework.

The main thing to avoid in any literature review is what might be called the 'card index' method, which consists of a dull and poorly organised sequence along the lines of, 'A said this ... B said that ... and C said ...'.

3.1.3 The Concluding Section

The role of the concluding section is simply to draw the paper to a close by restating the aims and then providing a strong clear statement of the major results. This section is not the place for lengthy comparisons with earlier literature or extensive discussion of 'policy implications', since these should appear in the main body of the paper. While the reader should be in no doubt about the contribution made by the paper, avoid making excessive claims. There is also no need to go into detail about ways in which the work can be extended. Try to avoid a final sentence which is left 'hanging in mid-air' or which stresses negative points.

3.2 The Appearance of a Research Paper

It is necessary to pay close attention to the 'mechanics' of producing a paper; this not only ensures that the resulting paper looks like a professional piece of work, but makes life easier for the reader. For example, it is necessary to be consistent in the use of titles and numbering systems, so that the reader always knows the status of a particular heading. Make decisions regarding the following aspects at an early stage. It can be very time consuming to make changes later.

In making these decisions, there are few unambiguously correct ways, for example, to number sections. What is important is consistency in the use of a chosen style. However, all publishers of books and journals, and organisations which issue research reports, have their own 'house style' to which authors must adhere. Compliance with an imposed style is often made easier by the use of 'templates' or 'styles' used by word processors.

3.2.1 Titles and Numbers

Most papers are unlikely to need more than three levels of titles. These are the main title of the paper, section titles (numbered 1, 2, ...), and subsection titles (numbered 1.1, 1.2, ...). Sometimes, subsubsection titles (numbered 1.1.1, 1.1.2, ...) may be needed. There is a vast choice of options here. First, a numbering system is needed, involving either arabic or roman (capital or lower case) numbers, or even alphabetical schemes. Always use a consistent font, capitalisation, spacing and position (either centred or against the margin), so that the reader immediately identifies the status of the title. Keep the titles succinct but meaningful and avoid terse generic titles like 'model', 'data' and 'results'. The first sentence after the title should not simply allude to the concepts used in the title.

Number all tables and figures and give them succinct descriptive titles. Refer to all tables and figures in the text. Again, a house style specifies a numbering system and convention for titles (above or below tables and figures) which must be followed. Do not crowd the tables too much. If the information is hard to fit into the table, it is usually better to divide it into two separate tables. Give columns clear headings. Above all, remember that numbers do not speak for themselves. You need to guide the reader to the most salient points.

Number all equations, even if you do not refer to them. The numbers are useful when other researchers wish to make reference to the equations. House styles have particular requirements concerning the layout of equations, whether against a margin, indented or centred, and the position of numbers (and style used, for example whether separate numbers are used within sections or whether they are numbered continuously throughout the paper).

3.2.2 Notes and Appendices

Use appendices for things like extensive data descriptions, longer derivations of analytical results, and subsidiary analytical or empirical results. These may otherwise interrupt the flow of the paper too much or upset the 'balance' of various sections. Do not use appendices to define notation. As with most aspects of layout, there is no single correct method and the 'house style' determines whether appendices are placed before or after the list of references.

Use footnotes for groups of references to literature, or qualifications of the main argument, or small details which would otherwise interrupt the argument and which are not crucial for its development. Do not break a sentence with a footnote flag and do not place more than one footnote flag together at the end of a sentence. Depending on the house style requirements, endnotes may be used instead of footnotes. This may well affect their use, as it is easier for the reader to glance to the bottom of the page than to keep turning to the end of the paper.

Be sparing in the use of footnotes. The temptation to add lots of footnotes has sometimes been referred to as 'foot-and-note disease'. Keep in mind that if you really want the reader to look at the material in a footnote, put it in the text of the paper instead. One sign that a paper is from a postgraduate thesis is that there are too many long footnotes crowded with irrelevant citations and unnecessary discussion. As the American writer Frank Sullivan commented, 'give a footnote an inch and it will take a foot'.

3.2.3 References and Citations

A consistent style must be used when citing other works. For example, a popular style involves the name, or names, of authors followed by the date and, if necessary, the page numbers in parentheses. For example, a citation to Adam Smith's *Wealth of Nations* would take the form, 'Smith (1776, p. 210) suggested that ...'. If there are three or more authors, use only the first; for example, 'Jones *et al.* (1998) showed that ...'.[1] If the same author has more than one piece with the same date, use, for example, 'Marshall (1890a) ...' and so on.

Ensure that quotations are accurate and give precise page references for all quotations, however small they are. It is unfortunately very easy for inaccuracies to creep into quotations. Do not alter quotations by, for example, adding

[1] The terms *ibid, loc cit* and *op cit* are no longer used in the economics literature.

emphasis (italics). Avoid, wherever it is possible, using ellipses (...), particularly if the material omitted is part of the argument in the quoted material, as distinct from an allusion or reference. Many house styles suggest that if quotations are three or more lines in length, they should be placed in a separate indented paragraph.

All bibliographical details should be placed in the list of references, arranged alphabetically by author. The list must be complete and accurate, but should include only those items cited in the paper. A consistent style must be used regarding capitalisation, italics, initials, pagination, punctuation and ordering of material. The production of the list of references requires much more time than most authors imagine. An alarming variety of styles is used, and there seems to be no limit to the imagination of publishers and editors in devising their own unique house style. However, it is important, having settled on a style, to be consistent. Later changes can be time consuming.

3.2.4 Some Proprieties

Many aspects of research papers, such as the styles used for headings, citations and bibliographies, and arrangement of material, as discussed above, involve choices, although they may sometimes be imposed by house styles. However, there are some things that *must* be done to satisfy the minimum requirements of scholarship. These are listed here. Some of these points could well be arranged under the golden rule, *Do Not Plagiarise!*

1. Always acknowledge earlier work on which you have built. Give precise sources of the results, diagrams and equations of other authors.

2. State explicitly when you are summarising other people's arguments. This also helps you to be clear about precisely how you have made modifications and original contributions.

3. For all data sources, full details must be given, including page numbers. It must be possible for someone to replicate your results with the minimum of effort in obtaining the same data. Keep fully documented data files in case you are asked to make the data available to other researchers. Similarly, documented computer programs should be retained.

4. Acknowledge any help received while conducting the research or writing and revising the paper. However, acknowledge *only* those who have helped (not those to whom you have sent an earlier copy and who politely replied that they would 'waste no time' in reading the paper). Avoid adding the tiresome and unnecessary caveat that, 'all remaining errors are the responsibility of the author'. This is of course distinct from a disclaimer which may need to be included, where it is stated that the views do not represent an employer or organisation.

3.2.5 The Front Matter

All research papers and reports require some kind of front matter. As a minimum, this consists of a title page giving the title, the authors and their affiliation, and perhaps acknowledgements to colleagues or research grants. It may also contain an abstract. The abstract consists of a single paragraph (usually no more than about 300 words) stating the aims of the paper and perhaps major results. Sometimes a house style requires a table of contents, and perhaps separate lists of tables and figures, with the corresponding page numbers. The front matter may also include keywords. A house style also indicates rules for pagination, such as whether the front matter should be numbered separately.

3.3 The Writing Process

This section discusses the process or craft of writing, rather than the mechanics and appearance of a paper. As stated earlier, the aim of writing is to achieve clarity. Getting a paper looking right is largely a matter of following a set of conventions, but clear writing is very difficult. There is no point in doing research unless it can be communicated to other people.

Clear writing requires great care and a capacity to read one's own work as if it had been written by someone else. This is helped by leaving the finished product alone for a while. A main aim is to avoid writing 'balderdash', sometimes called gobbledygook. The famous economist Jacob

Viner (1958, p. 377) referred to two basic types of balderdash.[2] The first, simple balderdash, arises where the author believes that he or she understands, but cannot make it intelligible to the reader. The second type, called compound balderdash, comes in two varieties. In one variety, neither the author nor the reader can make any sense of the text, and in the second variety the reader thinks he or she understands but the author knows it is meaningless. It is frightening to realise just how easy it is to produce examples of these types. Vigilance is always needed, even by experienced writers.

Another type of writing, or more strictly thinking as it is quite different from balderdash, to be avoided is what Jeremy Bentham called 'nonsense on stilts'. This is the special type of pseudo-sophisticated nonsense and ignorance which only the educated are capable of producing and reading without horror, and which the uneducated immediately recognise as ludicrous.

3.3.1 Some Writing Basics

The nonlinear nature of research has already been stressed: a significant amount of rewriting must be expected. Indeed, perhaps the most important rule of writing is that the first draft is not the final draft but is simply the start of a long process of revision. But this process need not be painful. Indeed, it can be pleasant and rewarding. It is remarkable how small changes to crucial expressions, or minor

[2] He alluded to an unidentified 'eighteenth century French wit' as his source.

rearrangements of material, can substantially improve the clarity of a paper.

Much benefit can usually be gained by asking friends or colleagues to read a draft. But do not inflict on them a 'half baked' draft that you know is incomplete or sloppy. Use the spell-checker before handing it over, and do not expect everyone to read it with the same interest. Be careful to select people you know to be sympathetic and constructive, as anyone can find negative things to say, however good the paper. As George Canning, the 19th century British Prime Minister, pleaded, 'save me from the Candid Friend'. However, do not try to defend the indefensible. Do not fall in love with your own writing. Be willing to respond to suggestions.

A first requirement in writing anything, whether it is a research paper or a novel, is that the author needs to form a clear view of the reader. Never 'talk down' to the reader. A certain amount of knowledge must be assumed, but be careful to avoid being too allusive. Above all do not address only your fellow experts in the topic. There is always a danger of talking to one's self. After living with a research project for some time, it is perhaps easy to forget that most other people are not as familiar with the literature as you are. It is sometimes useful, in getting the level right, to imagine that you are giving a seminar presentation to your peers. Giving a seminar is a good way to expose ideas and concentrate the mind. Even if it does not elicit many comments, the experience can suggest revisions needed to the paper.

3.3.2 The Importance of an Outline

At a very early stage in the research, draw up a detailed table of contents. This is by no means a trivial task, as working out the arrangement of material is often complex, particularly at a stage when little of substance has been achieved. The table should contain as much detail as possible, including section and subsection titles. This plan allows you to see the sequence of the argument at a glance (this sequence may of course be quite different from the research plan, discussed above). The writing will not necessarily move linearly from the start to the end, and having a clear view of the arrangement makes it possible to write in the most convenient order while keeping the overall shape in mind.

3.3.3 Some Hints for Clear Writing

It cannot be said too often that the first draft will not be the last. There is a story of a visitor to an English stately house asking how the splendid lawns are produced. The answer was simply to sow the seed and then weed and roll it for five hundred years. An analogy can be drawn with good, clear writing. It is necessary to go over what you have written many times.

Remember too that length is not a measure of quality. The American writer Mark Twain once wrote, 'I would have made this letter shorter, but I didn't have the time.' Writing can vary from verbose, through succinct to terse. Only a succinct style is desirable, but it is not easy to get the balance right. Often some well-chosen cuts can reduce the length while at the same time improving the flow of a sentence. For example, consider the following sentence.

> I have found from experience that it is usually quite possible, at a later stage, simply to remove unnecessary words, which unfortunately clutter up the text without adding subtantive content, such that further awkward rearrangements to the structure of the sentence do not need to be made.

This can easily be reduced to the simple statement that, 'it is usually possible to remove unnecessary words without making further rearrangements'.

The following hints may be useful in achieving clarity.

1. Re-read as you go along. In particular, before turning to a new paragraph, read the previous one. Before starting a new writing session, re-read the previous work. This will help to improve continuity. Regularly check the linkages between sections.

2. Stop writing while at a convenient point when it is going well. Simply jot down a few notes and keywords as reminders. If the writing is going well, resist the temptation to keep going until you have reached the end of the particular section, or you have exhausted

your current ideas. By stopping before reaching that point, you will find it much easier to pick up the work the next day and start again, knowing how it needs to proceed.

3. When reading through what you have written, try to produce a succinct summary of each paragraph. This will help to determine whether a subtitle is needed, or whether you should change the order of the material, or whether anything needs to be added to improve continuity or clarity. Ask yourself if it is repetitive. If you cannot summarise the paragraph, delete it.

4. Be gender neutral. This can easily be achieved without mixing singular and plural, as in 'an individual who maximises their utility', or over-using 'he or she'.

5. In reporting earlier work by other researchers, use the past tense (as in, 'economist X found that ...'). In indicating the contents of your later sections, use the present tense (as in, 'section X reports estimates of ...'). However, use the past tense in the concluding section.

3.3.4 Things to Avoid

A research paper is not meant to be read aloud or to entertain the reader. It should be written in a calm and clear manner so that the emphasis is always on the issue at hand. Some suggestions of features to avoid are listed here.

1. Avoid colloquial, conversational or highly personalised expressions. These provide colour to speech but are out of place in research papers.

2. Avoid abbreviations (such as &, don't and etc.) and avoid overusing acronyms.

3. Avoid overusing personal pronouns (I, we, you, me).

4. Avoid antiquated, verbose, pedantic and pompous language.

5. Do not be allusive.

6. Do not annoy the reader by making gratuitous negative remarks about other researchers' work. Such negative comments can easily lead to a loss of sympathy on the part of the reader, even if other people are being criticised. Instead, make direct and precise statements about how your work differs from previous analyses and 'accentuate the positive'. After all, it is easy to be destructive and to find fault, but hard to be constructive.

7. Avoid an excessive use of adjectives and adverbs. When editing your first draft, look out in particular for 'very', 'extremely' and 'highly', which are usually best deleted. In addition, 'had' can often be deleted (as in 'they had examined ...'). Avoid using 'it can be noted that', 'it is important to stress that' and 'it is of interest that'.

8. Do not use metaphors, which usually add colour at the expense of clarity.

9. Avoid writing content-free sentences (this trap seems to be particularly hard to avoid when writing introductions).

10. Avoid using bullet points. These may be convenient for notes or lecture presentations, but are out of place in a paper, which requires a continuous narrative with a clear logical sequence.

11. It hardly seems necessary to add the advice to avoid clichés like the plague.

3.4 Checklists

This section contains two sets of checklists. The first takes the form of a list of questions, while the second set is a list of reminders, which may be consulted before completion of the 'first complete draft'.

3.4.1 The Structure of the Analysis

1. Is the problem clearly stated?

2. Are hypotheses and assumptions explicit?

3. Is the relationship to previous work made clear?

4. Are the limitations acknowledged?

5. Are the data fully described and their precise sources given?

6. Are the conclusions explicitly stated?

3.4.2 The Basic Appearance of the Paper

1. Format: Check the preliminaries, title pages and contents pages.

2. Headings: Check the consistency of style, fonts, numbering and spacing.

3. Quotations: Check their accuracy and page references. A large proportion of quotations are inaccurate.

4. Tables: Check titles, abbreviations and details needed for interpretation and cross-references.

5. Equations: Check numbering and cross-references.

6. References: Are all cited works included? Do not include any items which are not cited. Are works in alphabetical order? Is the style consistent? Are all details, such as volume number, page numbers, date, place of publication and publisher, given?

3.5 Conclusions

This chapter has stressed the need to communicate research results as clearly as possible. It is the author, rather than the reader, who needs to do the really hard work of simplifying as much as possible and expressing ideas in a straightforward and transparent manner. Even the ideas of Edgeworth, one of the most famous economists of all, were slow to be widely appreciated and adopted, largely because his writing was directed to such a narrow audience. Edgeworth introduced the now-ubiquitous concepts of indifference curves and the contract curve, along with the eponymous box diagram, in his highly original book on *Mathematical Psychics*. When reviewing this book, Jevons (1881, p. 582) commented that:

> The reader is left to puzzle out every important sentence like an enigma ... they would be puzzled out if some great pecuniary matter ... depended upon their comprehension. But social science has not yet taken such a rank that students feel bound to master any new truths propounded.

His argument, that authors need to work hard to make their work clear because the incentive to understand an opaque economic argument is small compared with a legal case involving large sums of money, is just as valid today as it was in 1881.

Highly experienced writers are capable of occasionally writing sentences containing one of the two types of balderdash described above, or even forgetting to mention their key findings and assumptions. Writing is a craft, and drafts must be edited and polished many times, paying close attention to detail as well as the overall shape and flow of the argument.

Jacob Viner, one of the most severe of critics, once commented in a book review that:

> The book before us is marked throughout by rigorous economy of verbiage, precision of expression, unadorned but none the less graceful simplicity of expression. The severity of the style is engagingly softened here and there by skillful turns of phrase.[3]

This is praise indeed, and describes qualities for which all authors can at least aim. In developing a style of writing research papers, a great deal can be learned by close study of authors who are particularly clear. All writers begin by imitating a style they strongly admire and find attractive, but of course ultimately they need to find their own 'voice'. However, be warned that, as the jazz musician Miles Davis once said, 'sometimes you have to play a long time before you learn to sound like yourself'.

[3]This is from Viner (1958, p. 265).

Part III

Working on a PhD

Chapter 4

The PhD Journey

The aim of this chapter is to offer some advice to help make the PhD journey pleasant and rewarding, with as little stress as possible. Although students clearly understand what is involved in doing the coursework component, starting a PhD thesis is typically a leap in the dark. This naturally leads to anxieties. While such a substantial project should not be taken lightly, and it cannot be denied that doing research is hard work and has inevitable frustrations, I believe that it should largely be a pleasant and rewarding experience. Students should gradually acquire a substantial range of skills and, above all, obtain an understanding of the standards required of scholarship and eventually develop the crucial ingredient of confidence in their ability to take on a research project.

Section 4.1 considers the nature of a PhD thesis. The selection of a topic is discussed briefly in section 4.2. Section 4.3 considers some aspects of life as a PhD student and features associated with working towards a thesis. Section 4.4 makes some suggestions regarding an approach to tackling such a large project, involving breaking it down into smaller components. The important role of the supervisor is then discussed in section 4.4.1. Some suggestions regarding non-PhD activities are made in section 4.5.

4.1 What is a PhD?

Research is a process of making discoveries. These may be new empirical regularities, new theoretical insights and an improved understanding of economic problems. A PhD as a research degree therefore needs to say something quite new, rather than collating or rehearsing existing knowledge. This presents a difficult challenge. Contrary to a popular illusion, such progress is largely achieved by making a series of small steps, rather than taking giant leaps. A distinguishing feature of research is that it is the researcher who formulates the precise questions to be examined and decides on the approaches used. Indeed, the clear specification of the problem is an important element in planning a project. The question has to be clearly defined and seen to be worthy of attention. Eventually, you should be able to state clearly what you have contributed to knowledge.

The understandable tendency to look at the final destination instead of the closer road ahead is reflected in the first question often asked by PhD students. They want to know what is expected of them – what do they have to do to get their PhD? The standard answer is of course that a PhD is normally described as containing material for three publishable papers.[1] This response is nevertheless both vague and an oversimplification. The thesis should have a central 'core' or theme which ties the separate contributions together, although the closeness between topics differs significantly among theses. There is a huge variation in the quality of theses produced, even within the same university department. What all students need to aim for is a high standard of work which can be recognised as demonstrating a mature approach to research.

4.2 Selecting a Topic

Most students have a broad idea of the area of research they would like to pursue. This may come from previous reading required for coursework or it may be stimulated by attending research seminars. But in deciding on a PhD topic the first step is to refine the statement of the problem, in particular to narrow the scope of the project so that it is more clearly defined and manageable. Some aspects of this section obviously overlap with, and repeat, the discussion in chapter 2 above. As part of this process it is extremely important for you to be able to express the topic in the form of an explicit question: if this cannot be done, it is likely that the subject is not well defined. The initial temptation, to be strongly resisted, is to raise 'big' questions which would occupy a lifetime of research.

[1] However, in practice few theses actually lead to publications.

The process of arriving at a clear question and hence starting point begins in the library. The process of investigating the literature has been considerably eased by the existence of computer search facilities. But great care needs to be taken in using these aids. Only a familiarity with the subject can provide an indication of the keywords that are likely to be fruitful. Some bibliographic databases are limited to journals (and necessarily only a selection of these), so that important contributions in books may be overlooked. There is no alternative to getting your hands dirty in a library. Examine the relevant journals and follow up the references given in the articles to other work which appears relevant. During this stage you will need to develop an idea of which journals are most important and who are the major contributors to the area of research.

When carrying out the preliminary reading, it is important always to ask yourself questions – do not simply read passively. The types of question are as follows. Can the approach used in a study be applied to other contexts, countries or time periods? What assumptions are implicit? Are all the assumptions sensible? To what extent might the results be sensitive to the assumptions? How can they be relaxed? Are there any unnecessary assumptions? Is the approach used the most appropriate one? Have new techniques been developed since the paper was written? Have all relevant statistical tests been carried out? Are the results consistent with expectations, or earlier work? Are the surrogate or constructed variables the most appropriate for the task and can anything be said about likely biases? Are there any implications of the study which have not been fully drawn out by the author? Can these be exploited in your work? In thinking about possible extensions to applied work it will be necessary to check if necessary datasets are available.

Your supervisor will be important in influencing the way you begin. But do not expect a supervisor to place a topic in your lap. Finding a research subject is your responsibility.

A supervisor will nevertheless lead you towards getting a clear focus to start the first paper, and will form a judgement about whether there is likely to be 'mileage' in any suggested topic. Various simplifications or types of modelling strategy may be suggested, and your supervisor may offer valuable warnings against initially taking on too much. In describing what you want to investigate, you should be able to frame a clear question. In these early stages when you are reading widely, your supervisor is likely to ask questions such as, 'what was the question motivating this paper?', 'what are the author's major results?', 'what do you regard as the main limitations of the approach?', and 'in what ways do you expect your research to extend existing literature?' Be prepared to answer those questions.

In some cases a supervisor may suggest starting your PhD by working jointly on a well-defined topic. You can learn a lot from closely seeing your supervisor working. But if working with a supervisor, you should discuss the question of authorship right at the beginning. Ask directly by saying something like, 'do you have in mind producing a joint paper under both of our names and, if so, would the names be listed in alphabetical order?' It is nevertheless very important that this kind of direction changes in nature. If you are given such a start, you must 'run with it'. You should independently chase up further literature and constantly be on the look-out for ways in which extensions could be made. You need to offer your own constructive suggestions. Eventually you will be on your own. However, universities have different regulations regarding the use of joint work, so it is important to check your own university rules.

4.3 Life as a PhD Student

Life as a PhD student is completely different from that experienced as an undergraduate, so this section offers some general advice about research on a thesis.

4.3.1 Costs and Benefits

First, no one should be under any illusion – completing a PhD thesis is hard and at times exhausting work. It will involve long hours of tedious work. Some inviting avenues will turn into dead ends. Going down a dead end for a while should not be considered as wasted time, as it is a normal part of research and valuable insights are usually gained. But judgement is needed about the time to turn back and try a different route: again this is where the supervisor's judgement can help. There will be times of despondency where it seems that nothing worthwhile is going to be achieved. Research is hard, and often comes with occupational hazards like sleepless nights and bad headaches. Many sacrifices need to be made. But at the same time it should be highly rewarding. There is a considerable sense of achievement and often excitement in making progress with a research project. To anyone with intellectual curiosity – surely the first important ingredient needed for research – the ability to carry out a substantial piece of original research is a privilege. The freedom to pursue a subject of special interest over a long period is of great value.

It is also worth keeping in mind that for the vast majority of people, the period of PhD study is the only time in their life when it is possible to pursue a concentrated piece of research in one area, without the other heavy responsibilities and endless deadlines and interruptions which come with employment. Although work for a PhD may appear to involve much pressure, after full-time graduate work virtually no one has the luxury of devoting all their energy to a single piece of work. This fine opportunity should never be wasted – lost time cannot be recovered.

It is also for most students a period in life which is marked by a rapid growth in understanding and increased maturity. The ability to absorb new material and learn new skills is great. This all brings its rewards – of a non-pecuniary kind in addition to the standard returns accruing to investment in education and training.

4.3.2 The Working Routine

It is important to start the PhD journey by establishing good research and organisational habits. Develop a disciplined working routine regarding the organisation of your time. Your commitment should be at least that of a full-time job. Plan each working day's tasks before you even arrive at the office or library. Have a daily working schedule, including a fixed starting time each morning. Above all, write as you go along.

Always keep full bibliographical information about the papers and books you consulted. Record all details of data sources used and any adjustments you might make. If you produce any computer programs, provide lots of comments and write brief documents describing how to use the programs, including how the input data must be arranged.

Decide right at the beginning which word processing package you prefer to use, and develop the appropriate formats and styles, bearing in mind that any separate papers you produce will eventually form the basis of one or more chapters: all these things are tedious to change at a later stage. At an early stage, check with your Graduate Office regarding any special style requirements. Keep materials in well-organised folders rather than in piles on your desk or floor. Regularly make several digital backups of everything, and store them in different locations.

4.4 The Journey as a Sequence of Steps

Instead of thinking of the substantial challenge ahead – akin to climbing a mountain – it is advisable to think in terms of taking just one step at a time. Put the final destination of the journey out of your mind. It is not possible anyway to anticipate at the outset precisely where work on a thesis is likely to lead. There are several benefits of beginning simply with the idea of writing one paper, even though it will be seen as leading to further research. One important role of the supervisor is obviously to judge whether there is likely to be further 'mileage' in the topic: this is where the supervisor's research experience and judgement are helpful.

One of the hardest problems facing students is to learn to appreciate the standards needed: the importance of mastering this cannot be exaggerated. Eventually you must be able to view your own work critically and realistically, as if it had been written by someone else. Sometimes the strongest students actually undervalue what they have produced, and need to be encouraged not to throw it out, but more usually the difficult problem is to realise when more work needs to be done. Much of this learning can be achieved during the writing of a first paper.

There are many skills – not least of which is the ability to write clearly – required to produce a mature paper. It is likely that this first paper will involve the greatest struggle of any part of the thesis. Compared with some other disciplines, results in economics often come slowly and it can take some time to develop a clear understanding of just what has been achieved. You may wonder when your supervisor will finally stop telling you to make revisions. Importantly you will wonder when your own understanding of precisely what you have contributed, and how it fits into the wider literature, will stabilise. But avoid the temptation to become impatient to get on with something new. Above all, do not leave the paper in a 'nearly complete' state with the idea of going back to it. It is very important to get into the habit of finishing things.

You will of course go back to the paper later, but important lessons are learnt in first getting it to a standard where it can be circulated. After successfully accomplishing this first stage, most students find that the next papers are produced much more quickly and with far fewer problems. With a decent paper, you are also in a position to present seminars and workshops, which can be valuable for producing feedback and meeting other people with similar interests. The discipline and concentration needed to prepare and give a seminar are also valuable.

The elusive but highly desirable quality needed for the PhD journey is that of 'momentum'. With this quality, one piece of research will naturally lead to another – although, understandably, this may seem unlikely for those just setting out. Indeed, if things are going well, a crucial role of the supervisor is to call things to a halt. A point will be reached where the supervisor can say, 'OK, it is splendid that you can see all these interesting places to go, but you have to stop here and consolidate everything.' It is much more comfortable to be told that you have in fact nearly reached this (now limited) destination, than constantly to be in a state of anxiety about whether the finish line will ever come into sight.

Once this point is reached, you can then review the various papers and, with advice from your supervisor, work out what is needed to prepare the thesis itself. The papers can be organised, and sometimes divided, into chapters. It should be clear where additional material, such as introductions and linking material, is needed. The relative 'weight' of different sections will also become evident and may need adjustment. Decisions can be made about moving material to or from appendices.

The complete work can then be polished and improved by the addition of various elaborations, cross-references and further signposts. In doing this you will learn to handle a large manuscript, while having the pleasure of seeing all the work come together in a single integrated document. This last stage is pleasant and quite relaxing, but it cannot be completed quickly.

Many students are given the impression that they must write a 'literature review' chapter, but this is not correct. This is fortunate as a good literature review is extremely hard to produce. However, the thesis must demonstrate an awareness of the relevant literature and the reader must be able to see clearly how the thesis extends existing work. But this does not mean that a separate chapter is necessarily required. Indeed, it is usually much better to refer to most earlier work at appropriate points in the development of your own analysis, and in motivating the approach adopted and the questions asked. This also helps to make it clear to the reader precisely where your work departs from established work: a very common fault of many PhD theses is that such points of departure are not made explicit. Here, I am not ruling out the inclusion of a literature review which helps to motivate the thesis, if it is done well. But it is usually the weakest part of a thesis. You should of course begin to produce a bibliography at the start of your research.

4.4.1 Working With Your Supervisor

The route to a PhD thesis has many dangers, disappointments and dead ends, as well as high vantage points offering splendid views and fresh perspectives. Always remember, especially in the hard times, that you are not alone. You have the encouragement, support and guidance – with sometimes a restraining influence – of your supervisor. The importance of your supervisor cannot be exaggerated. This section is written as if there is just one supervisor, but some students have joint supervisors. Nevertheless, there is usually more contact with one of them, though the weights may vary over time. In the early stages, particularly involving the choice of a precise research question, meetings will usually involve both supervisors. It is always necessary to keep both people fully informed about your progress.

4.4.2 The Choice of Supervisor

The choice of supervisor is so important that you should always endeavour to take the initiative. Consider the alternatives available and decide who you would like to be your supervisor. Do not be afraid to ask. The supervisor need not necessarily be working in the field you have in mind. Indeed, some people may welcome students with other interests. Expert knowledge of the specific field is only one of many characteristics of supervision, and it is usually possible for a supervisor to arrange for someone who is closer to the field to look at the work at various points. You will eventually become the expert in your field and your supervisor cannot be expected to know all the papers you have read, so ensure that you accurately report the contents of papers in any discussions.

In selecting a supervisor, do take care to avoid anyone who is known to be unhelpful, sarcastic or negative, or who communicates poorly. And avoid those who are not themselves productive. It is easy to obtain CVs these days from departmental web sites. Remember that at various times you will need to ask advice about things other than the thesis work, such as future jobs or dealing with difficult situations, so trust and sympathy are important.

4.4.3 The Working Relationship

It is necessary to establish a congenial working relationship with your supervisor, but there are few general rules about this. Each case is different depending on the personalities and abilities involved. A supervisor should be flexible. A good supervisor does not want to produce a disciple or clone, or a research assistant, but aims to help prepare students to make their own individual way and develop their own interests and style.

A good supervisor therefore treats each student differently, making a judgement about each student's abilities and character. For example, some students benefit by being pushed hard and being given regular tight deadlines. Other students work best when they are given more time and space to work at their own speed. Some students need more encouragement and moral support than others – often students become very anxious about their progress and need to be reassured, while others need prodding. A supervisor should not be miserly with praise but should also be clear if work is not up to standard.

There are also no rigid rules regarding the frequency of meetings with your supervisor. At the early stages, these are obviously likely to be more frequent but will vary. Nevertheless it is something that should be discussed explicitly and some universities actually have clear regulations about meetings. If your work is going well, it is useful just to keep your supervisor informed with a quick progress report. Make good use of your supervisor – the university is after all making a valuable scarce resource available to you. If you are having serious difficulties with an aspect of the research, such as obtaining empirical results or solving a difficult problem, or are anxious about whether a result is of any value, go to see your supervisor rather than struggling or worrying alone. It is often the case that a supervisor can 'cut through' the problem quickly or suggest an alternative approach.

4.4.4 Some Rules of Conduct

Although you will want to build a pleasant and trusting working relationship, you should actually be a little hesitant before approaching your supervisor. Think twice before asking anything. Before asking any question, always first ask yourself if you have done enough to answer it by yourself. Make sure you can explain the problem sufficiently clearly – rehearsing an explanation can often lead you to the answer. Ensure that you are fully prepared, so that you avoid wasting the time of someone who is inevitably very busy.

Always ask yourself if the work you are about to hand over could be better: ensure that you have done yourself justice. However, if you do not fully understand what your supervisor is asking you to do, ask for further clarification in order to avoid wasting time in the future.

There are some things you should not do regarding your supervisor.

1. Never look pained or unwilling to try suggested changes to the modelling specification or estimation method, or extensive revisions to drafts.

2. If you think your supervisor is wrong about something, do not argue but express your desire to try to rewrite your analysis more clearly for future discussion.

3. Do not take a pile of computer output and expect your supervisor to sieve through all the detail – you should abstract what is important first.

4. Do not ask your supervisor to read a scrappy or highly provisional piece of work (unless you are specifically asked to present a sketch or outline of a particular section).

5. Do not ignore, or treat lightly, suggestions regarding reading matter or modelling approaches: if you do so, you can expect to find that constructive suggestions simply come to an end and your meetings become rather short.

6. Do not ask to borrow your supervisor's books.

It is important to listen closely for hints from your supervisor. In many cases these may not be explicit or obvious. Your supervisor may simply be thinking aloud and saying something like 'that is curious', or 'I wonder if ...'. Follow up on any questions that you had difficulty answering. Also take an interest when your supervisor talks about other work or economists. Follow any allusions to books, economists or articles which are not familiar to you. In this way you will increase your breadth of knowledge. Indeed, it is often during digressions and discussions of epiphenomena that you can learn a great deal.

4.5 Non-PhD Activities

Work on a thesis involves sustained concentration – the second important ingredient needed for research – on a single piece of work. However, it is important to allocate time to keep up with background reading. This period is also the time to read widely in the vast broader non-textbook literature of economics – learn to place modern work in a wider perspective. Read biographies of famous economists. It may seem that such wider reading has to compete against time spent on the more urgent primary task of work on the thesis, but I believe it is complementary and worthwhile, and can be done after the more demanding work of the day.

It is tempting to do some teaching and PhD students are often encouraged to give tutorials or even lectures. But be very careful. It can take up far more time and, importantly, energy than is realised until it is too late. Graduate students are always over-optimistic about their ability to fit teaching into their work schedule.

Go to seminars, whatever the topic, to get an insight into the issues which interest other people and the way they go about their own work. Observe what makes their presentations successful. Good seminars can also be inspiring even if the topic is far removed from your own work. Talk to other students about their work and ask them to comment on your drafts. There was a time when PhD study involved a lonely existence. Graduate students were 'second class' citizens, had no resources and had to struggle to find a seat in the library to do their work. There were few others in the same situation with whom they could share experiences. All this has now changed.

It has been stressed that work on a PhD involves many hours of concentrated effort, but that the period of full-time graduate study should also be a period in which you can broaden your appreciation of economics. It is also important to spend time during this period reading even more widely. Turning to entirely different subjects can be a valuable distraction from a narrow piece of research and it helps to keep things in perspective. For example, this is a time to read high-quality literature and broaden one's tastes in music and other arts. Such wider reading will, furthermore, contribute towards the maturing process that is so important for producing a serious piece of work such as a PhD thesis.

Many graduate students also find that participation in regular sporting activities, or other non-intellectual pursuits, provides a valuable diversion from work. These are useful for their own sake and, after grappling with a difficult problem for some time, it is often possible to make more rapid progress following physical exercise. Sensible organisation of your time will allow room for such extra-curricula activities.

4.6 Conclusions

This chapter has suggested some ways in which the route towards a PhD thesis can be made more fulfilling and less stressful. It should be a hard but rewarding task, rather than one that is full of anxiety. It is perhaps natural for most students initially to focus on the final destination, but it is nevertheless important to appreciate that, as with many other aspects of life, it is really the journey that matters.

The ability to work on a PhD thesis is a golden opportunity to develop research skills, confidence and judgement. It should also be a period of wider personal development and growing maturity. Research towards a PhD is associated with the transition from being a student to working as a professional economist.

Part IV

Publishing Research

Chapter 5

Books and Journals Compared

It is perhaps tempting to believe that the hard work involved in producing research ends with the completion of a manuscript. In reality, the path from manuscript to publication can present many hazards and involves a new and quite different type of learning process. The various stages of the publication process are designed to act as a selection device, or filter, and to improve the quality of the final product itself. Without these features it is likely that many more articles and books would contain serious errors or material that is unclear or directed to a narrower audience than necessary. Of course, no filter can be perfect and it is not difficult to find examples where the process has worked badly.

The aim of this part of the book is to indicate some of the main features of the publication process, so that readers may be in a better position to make judgements about published work and writers may be, to some extent at least, prepared to face the difficulties that inevitably lie in their path. The present chapter compares books and journals, while the following chapter concentrates on the process involved in getting papers accepted for publication in journals. While some of the features of publishing are common to all disciplines, there are important differences, and these chapters, like the rest of the book, are specifically intended for economists.

Much has been written about the many facets of the publication process. For a collection of papers on publishing in economics, see Gans (2000). Regarding book publishing, the famous description and memoirs of Unwin (1926, 1960) are still worth reading, despite the revolutions in printing technology and the structure of the industry that have since taken place. For a collection of publishing anecdotes, see Huggett (1986).

First, comparisons between books and journals are made in section 5.1, concentrating on the aims of, and constraints imposed on, editors which influence their behaviour. Section 5.2 discusses the growth in the number of journals. These two sections provide a broader context for discussing appropriate publication strategies for authors, as well as indicating to readers why the styles of books and journals are so different and why, for example, journal articles are usually so terse.

5.1 Books and Journals

The major forms of publication for research work are books and refereed journals. Other forms include departmental working papers, pamphlets, reports and other non-refereed forms, along with the more recently introduced form of 'on-line' publishing. For discussion of the latter possibilities, many of which have since been put in practice, see Goffe and Parks (1997). Without doubt the most important people, at least from the point of view of authors, are the editors. Hence a useful way to describe the main characteristics of these forms of publication is to begin by contrasting the nature of the editors themselves, and their quite different modes of behaviour and editorial policies. When discussing books here, the term editor is used instead of the more cumbersome 'commissioning editor'. At one time, editors played a significant editorial role, particularly with non-academic works. A distinction also needs to be made regarding 'contributed' volumes (including festschrifts and conference volumes), which are not discussed here.

5.1.1 The Aims of Editors

It is first necessary to stress that the main aims of book and journal editors are quite different. Put baldly, journal editors are looking for articles that have something new and worthwhile to say while book editors are looking for something that will sell. Originality is the primary requirement of a journal article, the success of which is judged by the number of subsequent citations and the enhanced reputation of the journal and, of course, the author. Journals publish literature reviews, but these require a fresh perspective and the synthesis of often disparate threads, along with the exercise of judgements regarding methods and directions of research.

The first question of book editors is not 'is this original?' but 'will this sell?' Of course, editors also like to have books that will enhance the quality of their lists, and perhaps attract other authors, but the market test is the crucial one. The lack of concern for originality is obvious in the case of textbooks, though of course a fresh style of exposition and perspective play a significant role. However, research volumes (usually referred to as monographs) may include material that the author has previously published in journal form.

In view of changes to the academic reward system which have substantially reduced the incentive to publish books, it is less likely that authors are prepared to publish original material only in a book. But the results of a substantial research programme, having a unifying theme, can often usefully be revised and brought together in a single volume after they have been published separately in a series of journal papers. It is also possible to include explanatory details and further discussion that could not be published in journal form. Such books are particularly valuable for later generations of researchers who are looking for an overview of a particular subject.

In economics, unlike several other disciplines, authors are usually required to sign forms giving the copyright to the journal. However, these agreements typically state that authors are entitled subsequently to use the work in a book published under their own name, without the need to obtain permission, subject to the original source being acknowledged.

5.1.2 Editors Compared

Many of the behavioural differences between journal and book editors become clearer once the motivating factors, and constraints, are recognised. First, journal editors are not paid employees, though some editors may receive a small honorarium. Many journal editors are appointed by some type of society, in much the same way that any other office bearer is appointed. Importantly, this means that there are no real sanctions regarding performance. It can be extremely difficult to remove a journal editor, however poor the performance or numerous the complaints made.

Journal editors are not selected according to their knowledge of the printing and publishing business, or even their administrative abilities. Many therefore know little, and care even less, about those aspects. If journal editors face no sanctions, have little knowledge of the technical and commercial aspects of publishing, and have no financial incentives regarding outcomes, it is inevitable that factors such as power, influence and ego play a role, thereby damaging the selection process. Many editors nevertheless do provide a valued and disinterested service to the scholarly community. It is perhaps surprising how well the system generally works, though there are huge variations in editorial standards.

Book editors are, in contrast, paid professionals whose remuneration depends on the sales of books they commission. There is thus a clear market sanction. There is indeed much mobility within the industry, as successful editors are 'headhunted'. This, combined with frequent take-overs, can have negative effects for individual authors – when there is no one to promote their book in the organisation. Commissioning editors typically know the publishing business well from many points of view, having often 'worked their way' through a number of departments.

The behaviour patterns of the different editors are therefore, not surprisingly, quite distinct. Journal editors simply wait for submissions to arrive.[1] With limited space available, emphasis is given to the selection process, involving the rejection of a large proportion of submitted papers. Rejection rates vary substantially among disciplines but are very high in economics. At the other extreme, law journals are largely edited by students, so there are few rejections. Publication and processing delays also vary substantially.

Editors are generally, though not always, well-known and often highly regarded academics. They are confident of their own ability to make judgements regarding the quality

[1]However, editors of new journals need to make an effort to get submissions, for which they often use 'special issues'.

of papers submitted, though an important role is played by referees, as discussed below. Furthermore, an editor may consult an editorial board before making a final decision, but this is not common. Journal editors have little, and merely distant, contact with authors. Given the search for original high-quality papers, past reputations of authors typically count for little. Furthermore, a double blind review process is now sometimes used so that the identity of authors is not meant to be known by referees. However, the identity of an author can usually easily be guessed or obtained simply by tracing an earlier version of the paper issued as a departmental Working Paper.

Book editors, on the other hand, must actively solicit manuscripts and proposals from potential authors.[2] They welcome submissions, but in approaching a publisher it is usually necessary to complete a detailed proposal form. Authors should never simply post a manuscript to a publishing house, but should take the trouble to find the name of an editor. Information for authors can usually readily be obtained from book catalogues and internet sites, from which proposal forms can also be obtained.

Unlike journal editors who give much of their attention to rejecting papers, book editors place most emphasis on encouraging authors, with the aim of increasing their lists. They make themselves known to academics by visiting departments and attending conferences. They are not, and make no claims to be, experts in the field. However,

[2]Certain university presses are less energetic in this regard.

they make it their business to find out about reputations (including not only academic qualities, but reliability and ease of dealing with authors). Referees of book proposals, and publishers' readers of finished manuscripts, are paid for their services and are encouraged to be constructive.

Book editors often establish long term relationships with authors. For samples of correspondence, in (mostly) non-economics publishing, see Nowell-Smith (1967), Wheelock (1950) and Roberts (1966). They are invariably pleasant, congenial people. Their aim is to help authors to produce books which will sell. They are not judgemental in the way that journal editors are, and are not threatened by others or affected by professional prejudices or jealousies of the kind that may sometimes influence decisions of journal referees and editors.

5.2 Journals: Demand and Supply

The most cursory glance at academic journals reveals a huge increase in the number of journals, with most of the newer journals in recent years being 'field' journals concerned with reasonably well-defined areas within the discipline. In addition, the majority of journals are published, marketed and distributed by established publishing houses. Indeed, some publishers have concentrated so much on journals that they now form the largest part of their business.

The demand side of journals includes both the demand by readers (fellow professionals and students) and the need for publishing outlets by researchers. The most obvious factor has been the growth of the economics profession itself, associated with the large increase in university numbers, and the associated growth of university libraries with funding to purchase journals. The stimulus provided by the growth of universities has also been enhanced by the 'publish or perish' imperative that exists. Academic appointments, reputation and promotion depend largely on journal publications.

The 'mainstream' journals, such as the *American Economic Review* and the *Economic Journal* which date from the end of the nineteenth century, are associated with the time when economists were becoming conscious of their professional status, distinct from other social or political studies, and felt the need to provide a new form of publication outlet for their work. In the earlier years, these journals also published work by individuals who were not attached to university economics departments.

The examples given above are of journals started by national associations, to which many economists working in the countries are expected to belong, and which organise annual conferences. Some other examples include the *Canadian Journal of Economics*, the *Scottish Journal of Political Economy* and the *Economic Record*. There are also regional organisations, as in the case of the *Southern Economic Journal*.

The large growth in the number of academic economists has also led to a considerable increase in the extent of specialisation. This has in turn given rise to a demand for more 'field journals' dealing with specific areas or research. The increased professionalisation of the subject was initially partly associated with the introduction of new analytical techniques. Initially, some economists found it difficult to publish their work in the existing journals and so launched their own journals, often connected with the formation of their own societies. Obvious examples of this type include the *Review of Economic Studies* and *Econometrica*, dating from the 1930s. In more recent years there are too many in this category to list.

Some journals are described as 'house journals'. These are not necessarily associated with specialist fields but are started by particular departments, or research institutes, eager to enhance their own publications. Examples include the journals produced by organisations such as the National Institute of Economic and Social Research (in the UK), the Melbourne Institute of Applied Economic and Social Research (in Australia), the Institute For Fiscal Studies (in the UK), the Brookings Institution, and the International Monetary Fund (in the US). However, they usually also accept submissions from researchers elsewhere.

Examples of long-established house journals include the *Journal of Political Economy* (Chicago), *Economica* (the London School of Economics), *Oxford Economic Papers* (Oxford), the *Manchester School* (Manchester), and the *Quarterly Journal of Economics* (Harvard). Their editors are always drawn from within the particular department, and not surprisingly the quality of articles varies substantially, even where the average quality of editors and papers is high.

On the supply side, publishers are attracted by the cash flow advantages of journals. Unlike books, where the uncertain returns accrue long after the expenses of paper, printing, binding, marketing and distribution have been incurred, journal subscriptions for a year ahead arrive at the beginning of the year. Not only are editors not paid, as mentioned above, but contributors receive no fee. Indeed some (though few) journals charge authors a cost per page, and many charge authors submission fees and impose costs for off-prints. Typically a publisher has a contract with, say, an economics society or research institute. These vary, but usually involve the payment of a minimum fixed amount by the publisher at the end of the year.

The burden of subediting and layout is sometimes borne (in terms of organisation and cost) by the society running the journal, but more often by the publisher. In recent years, further costs have been shifted to authors, who are now expected to provide camera-ready copy of diagrams, along with digital copies of papers laid out in an approximation to the journal's 'house style'.

Where a publisher is responsible for several journals, there are economies of scale regarding marketing and distribution. Furthermore, journals can provide a regular flow of work for a publisher's production department and (subcontracted) printers, which fill in any slack time. Journals do not take priority but allow some flexibility in scheduling work. Unlike books, where unsold copies are eventually pulped or remaindered, it is known from subscriptions approximately how many copies to print.

The above features also explain why journals have limited space and little flexibility. The subscription cost, and the agreement with the publisher, involves an explicit page limit per issue. It is important for each journal to have its own house style, involving page and font size, spacing, margins and other layout characteristics, along with paper quality and colour. These features cannot be varied to accommodate more or longer papers.

With books, there is much more flexibility and of course each book is priced separately. Nevertheless, a book contract will specify the approximate number of pages, and authors should endeavour to keep to this agreed length. Commissioning editors will have a view about the appropriate length and price for the market.

5.3 Conclusions

This chapter has provided a short description of the nature of books and journals. It has contrasted the different objectives and the behaviour of editors, in terms of the different incentives and constraints they face. The economics of book publishing and journal publishing are very different. Before considering any attempt to publish in either format, it is useful to invest some time in learning about the characteristics of different publishers and editors. This will save considerable time and inconvenience.

Chapter 6

Publishing in Journals

The previous chapter briefly contrasted books and journals as methods of publishing. The vast majority of researchers begin by publishing journal articles, and so this chapter concentrates on the special problems arising from the process of getting an article published in a journal. The various difficulties faced in this process and proprieties involved in publishing economics papers are discussed. The journey from submission of a paper to its eventual acceptance and publication is examined. The important first stage for the author, the journal choice and submission, is discussed in section 6.1.

There are really only two broad types of response from editors, and these are discussed. Section 6.2 considers the response to a rejection letter. The much more positive response – though it may not always seem so at the time – is the letter inviting revision and resubmission. This is discussed in section 6.3. Section 6.4 briefly concerns the role of sub-editors in the production process, and the importance of checking proofs carefully.

The broader subject of the various strategic aspects of writing and journal publishing is not discussed here. For discussion of these issues, see Fischer and Lawrence (1997). As this chapter is about the publication process, this is not the place to discuss the relative merits of different journals. However, early researchers would usually benefit from advice about the chances of publishing their paper in alternative journals, and the likely waiting times involved.

A point about the paper itself is worth stressing in this context. It is important not to be excessively negative about previous treatments of the topic or to emphasise originality by being provocative. This can annoy readers and, indeed, the very people being criticised may well be referees. Even disinterested readers find emphasis on negative points irritating, which may lead to a crucial loss of sympathy. A similar point was made by Hamermesh (1992), who also stressed the importance of not 'playing games' regarding acknowledgements and citations.

Furthermore, where the origins of a paper are in a thesis, substantial revisions are usually required before it is ready to be submitted to a journal. It must give all the indications of being a mature piece of work. Signs of immaturity, which are often evident in work taken from theses, include overlong and meandering introductions and conclusions, too many non-relevant citations, too many vague allusions, excessive claims for originality and policy relevance, long dense footnotes, and gratuitous criticisms of earlier work. Eliminate these features from your work before submitting.

6.1 Submission

One rule regarding journal submissions in economics stands out above all other requirements. The single most important propriety for authors to recognise is that a paper can be sent to only one journal at a time. The submission of a research paper contrasts with a book manuscript in this respect. Indeed, not only can a book manuscript be sent to several publishers (commissioning editors) simultaneously, but proposals – rather than the finished product – can be sent.

In view of the much greater investment of time involved in writing a book, many authors prefer first to obtain a contract, based on a proposal and perhaps some sample material. A book proposal needs to establish the existence of a likely market. The publisher takes a risk regarding the final quality, which is one reason why reputation is much more important in this context. Authors should be aware that contracts contain several clauses allowing the publisher to withdraw.

It should go without saying that before sending a paper to a journal, always ensure that it really is ready. Too often, editors receive papers that immediately convey – from their initial appearance or the opening paragraphs or state of tables, figures and references – all the wrong signals. Crucially, authors should try to obtain comments from sympathetic colleagues. They do not need to be experts in the area of the paper, but need to be willing to devote the time needed to give constructive advice. They can also advise against making extensive revisions to a draft that may not actually be required. University departments are much less collegial than they once were, and it is more difficult to get feedback from colleagues. But there is no doubt that those departments having some kind of editorial process for the release of their Working Papers enhance the publication chances of papers. Those who have made useful comments should of course be acknowledged but, in the words of Hamermesh (1992, p. 171), 'avoid the usual callow exculpation of them'. Never add acknowledgements to people who have not read the paper.

The first things the editor looks at are the title and the abstract, so it is important to make these as clear as possible. Despite this, many journal articles now often have highly allusive titles which give little indication of the subject of the paper, except perhaps to a small clique.[1] It is worth keeping later generations of readers in mind, for whom the allusions may mean nothing.

The journal should be selected carefully. Never send a paper to a journal without first looking through some

[1]Readers, including reviewers, of books should be aware that, in view of the market imperative, a publisher's marketing department often influences the title of a book. It is easy to discern fashions in titles. Non-academic histories and biographies now often refer to a minor feature of their subject. For example, a recent case, following the earlier example of Greene's *Lord Rochester's Monkey*, is *Lady Gregory's Toothbrush*.

recent issues to check if there are earlier related articles and whether it covers suitable fields and methods. Journals often provide a policy statement in their web site. Many papers are rejected without even being sent to referees because the editor immediately considers them unsuitable for the particular journal. It is also useful for inexperienced authors to seek advice on how well a prospective journal is edited. There are regrettably always some journals that are best avoided, unless one wishes to wait two or more years for a three-line rejection. The appendix to this chapter describes an example of rejection in terms, though in a different context, that will be familiar to anyone who has experience of submitting papers to journals.

Each journal has its own submission requirements, which need to be checked carefully. Submission is now often made easier by the ability to send pdf files as email attachments. When sending the paper, a brief formal covering letter of a couple of sentences is sufficient. The editor does not need to be told that the sender is looking forward to his or her response.

One of the first things authors need to develop is patience. In economics, the refereeing process can usually be expected to take a long time. The time between submission of the paper and a first response from the editor has without doubt increased in recent years: as an approximation, the median time is getting close to one year. Many authors would be horrified to discover how long their papers sit on an editor's desk before being sent to referees. Then when referees receive papers, they cannot be expected to give them high priority when all academics are under great pressure to produce their own work.

Almost the only incentive facing referees is a vague feeling that they are part of a community, and cannot expect to have their own work refereed seriously if they are not also prepared to contribute to the system. Hamermesh (1994) reported the results of a survey of journals regarding choice of, and behaviour by, referees. The summary statistics regarding turnaround times would almost certainly differ from current experience. Referees are seldom given a financial reward for their work and, when they are paid, the amount is trivial.

6.2 Dealing with Editors and Referees

The most frequent response from a journal editor is an unequivocal rejection. It is worth keeping this in mind when dealing with a rejection letter. Such rejections are much more common in economics than in most other disciplines. Indeed, many famous economics articles have been rejected by numerous journals. Many examples have been collected by Gans and Shephard (1994) and Shephard (1995). The most-published authors usually also necessarily have the most rejections along the way. The refereeing process introduces a substantial element of luck. Every author can easily think of some of their better papers which they have had great difficulty publishing, while some weaker papers have experienced few hurdles.

In dealing with rejections, it is necessary to find a balance between self-confidence, which is a fundamental prerequisite for any kind of research activity, and a willingness to learn from criticism. It is necessary, though never easy, to develop a thick skin. It is usually not difficult to think of those who need to develop a thinner skin, but this type is fortunately observed less frequently.

One point may take some time to appreciate. Despite the sometimes abusive and unkind comments, or frequently lazy and easy criticisms produced by referees, remember that it is not personal. A great deal could be written on the culture of negativity that has developed within the economics profession and the damage it has caused. Referees automatically look for things to criticise. But it is worth remembering that, after all, referees are human. There may be aspects of the paper that they find irritating, they are often very busy indeed and cannot spend time struggling with something that is unclear, they have their own little 'hobby horses', or they may simply have had a bad day. And in writing their reports they are of course protected by anonymity.

Also, keep in mind that after receiving a rejection, and possibly unpleasant referees' reports, it isn't the last chance: to borrow the often-quoted line of a famous film, 'tomorrow *is* another day'. The paper can be revised, there are other journals to which it can be submitted and the criticism is, after all, not public.[2] In this last aspect, a contrast may again be made with books, where the criticism comes after publication in the form of book reviews which, though usually signed, are much more public. Publishers may feel that there is no such thing as a bad review, but few authors would agree. It is worth remembering that reviewers often do not actually read books. The nineteenth century critic Sydney Smith once famously remarked, 'I never read a book before reviewing it; it prejudices a man so.'

Hence do not give up, unless a clear problem has been identified that cannot be rectified; this is rarely the reason for rejection. It is again useful to seek advice from an experienced colleague, who may be able to read 'between the lines' and suggest useful directions and priorities. Nevertheless, before sending it to another journal, keep in mind that the paper may need substantial revisions, involving a large amount of work. Never simply make further copies and submit an unchanged paper to another journal.

Above all, do not argue with or complain to the editor, even if the referees are wrong. In some cases, the referees may be positive about the paper, but it is still rejected by the editor for reasons that are far from clear. Again, there is no point engaging in any kind of correspondence with the editor. This point holds even when the referees' reports are instantly recognised as 'hatchet jobs'. This is a very

[2]However, I once saw a Working Paper where the author had included a rejection letter from a famous editor suggesting that the paper was the sort of thing that brings the profession into disrepute. After finally being published in another journal, it became a frequently cited paper.

short report designed only to give an excuse for rejecting a paper. Here the referee will pick on anything, most likely not the most vulnerable points of the paper, and say things like 'this is well known' and make other unsubstantiated and often incorrect comments.

Although it may be hard to deal with a rejection at the time, it is worth keeping in mind that much can often be learned from negative reports, and even those where the referee makes incorrect statements. These reports, if studied dispassionately, provide clues to help avoid future misinterpretations. They can show where assumptions have not been stated clearly or justified sufficiently, or even where the aims or implications of the work have not been expressed clearly. Often, rejection is a matter of the weight given to certain objections or qualifications, and the paper may not have argued convincingly where those qualifications may not affect the main results.

Common reasons for rejection are that the paper is not well motivated and its aims are not clear. This emphasises the need to pay special attention to the introduction, which often needs to be the most rewritten part of any paper. Another frequent reason for rejection is that, for various reasons, the contribution of the paper is simply not sufficient to warrant publication it that particular journal. This may well be an indication that it needs to be sent to a journal where it will face less competition, though even then it may first need more work.

6.3 Revise and Resubmit

An invitation to revise and resubmit is usually the best that can be expected. However, do not expect the editor to make complimentary remarks, or even appear to encourage resubmission. The wording is usually something like, 'we would be willing to consider a revision along the lines suggested by referees.' When finally accepting papers, most editors use the rather bland, 'your paper is now acceptable for publication'. Most editors seem congenitally unable to use the words 'sorry' or 'pleased'.

Editors and referees can sometimes be so opaque that a more experienced colleague may be needed to interpret the letter. Do not hesitate to show such letters to someone whose views you value. Such colleagues do not resent the time spent, and are simply passing on the type of advice from which they once benefited.

Do not expect referees to say kind things. In economics, even those who may like, or even admire, a paper feel obliged to concentrate on qualifications or other negative aspects. Nevertheless, the fact that a paper has not been rejected indicates at least a degree of sympathy on the part of the referees. Just a little bit of sympathy goes a long way and should be appreciated. Some inexperienced authors may feel discouraged by comments, when in fact they are relatively positive. After first reading the reports, it can be helpful to set them aside for a day or so before returning to them in a less sensitive frame of mind.

After receiving a 'revise and resubmit' letter, do not delay making revisions. It may often be difficult to return to a problem that is no longer fresh in the mind, and when new work appears more attractive: but revisions should be given priority. One non-trivial reason for avoiding delays is that the editor may change and the replacement may be less sympathetic and have different views about the direction of the journal. Returning to work on an older paper is made easier if decent records are kept, regarding for example computer programs written, data used or derivations of analytical results.

Deal with all the points made by the editor and referees. The editor's letter may indicate which points made by the referees are considered to be the most important, or which referee carries more weight. It is usually helpful to start by dealing with the most critical comments, as these lead to the most substantive changes, so that the minor comments may be dealt with 'along the way'. The revision process is likely to require several iterations to ensure that all points are covered.

Perhaps the most common requirement stipulated by an editor is to cut material: do not ignore this. Sometimes it is necessary to cut diagrams, blocks of material or a section of the paper. This is quite easy although it may be a little painful at first. More often a section needs to be shortened generally. The important point to realise is that compression – reducing unnecessary words and repetition – can usually be achieved while at the same time improving the flow and clarity of the paper.

Do not simply make the minimum changes demanded. Take the opportunity to look closely at the whole of the paper, even if referees do not ask for many changes, to see if the clarity of the argument can be improved. The time interval involved has the effect of placing a greater distance between the paper and the author, allowing for the important element of self-criticism. Authors need to take the attitude that a paper can always be improved. Indeed, the revision process often leads the author to gain a much better understanding of the strengths and weaknesses of the paper, and a realisation of its real contribution, thereby improving the focus and motivation.

When resubmitting the paper, carefully explain the modifications in a covering letter to the editor. The explanation should deal with each of the points made by referees, and if they are not numbered it is useful to add numbers to the paragraphs for easy reference. Do not simply state that a change has been made, but refer explicitly to the part of the paper where the revision occurs. If you believe that a point made by a referee is wrong or misplaced, give clear and politely expressed reasons. Remember that the most common explanation for a wrong interpretation is that the paper was not actually clear.

Sometimes referees differ about specific details and the editor does not indicate which one should be followed. In these cases, indicate the conflict and carefully explain the reasons for your choice. It is worth putting a draft letter aside for a couple of days: when returning to it, signs of irritation or an unpleasant tone may be clearer and thus expurgated.

Above all, do not assume that a revision, even where it seems that all points have been fully dealt with, will be accepted for publication. Keep in mind that the revision, along with the explanation to the editor, is likely to be returned to the original referees. More revisions may need to be made after further long delays and, even then, it is possible for papers to be rejected after going through several iterations. Some editors have a reputation for being less decisive than others.

6.4 The Production Process

An acceptance by the editor is by no means the end of the publication process. In economics, a further 18 months or two years often passes before the paper appears in print. During most of that time, the paper is simply waiting in a queue, but from the author's point of view the two important aspects are the contribution of sub-editors and the need to deal with proofs. These are discussed in turn in this section.

6.4.1 Sub-editors

An accepted paper is first sent to a sub-editor whose job is to ensure that it conforms with the journal's house style. The sub-editor will also 'mark up' the material for the person responsible for layouts. Of course, modern production methods do not require typesetting, or extensive retyping. Furthermore, checks are made to make sure, for example, that it has correct spelling and grammar, is consistent in its use of terms, and has all the bibliographical details needed. This process may give rise to 'author's queries', which may be dealt with by a separate communication between the production department and the author, or they may be included with the page proofs.

The extent of sub-editing of journal papers is usually 'light' and unobtrusive. The process is sometimes more intrusive with books. Given the difficulty of dealing with a large manuscript with multiple chapters and many references, inconsistencies are more easily introduced. Some sub-editors can appear to be authors manqué, and it is necessary to watch for changes in meaning introduced by a small rewording.

A good sub-editor can make a valuable contribution in eliminating any ambiguities and making sure that the references to table numbers or sections of a paper are the correct ones. Sub-editors may suggest improvements to the headings and layout of tables which improve their transparency. It is horrifying to realise the extent to which authors can introduce minor, but potentially confusing, differences between numbers mentioned in the text of a paper and a table. Good sub-editors are perhaps undervalued by authors and journal editors alike, who often remain ignorant of the many details that need to be considered if the journal is to retain a consistent style and quality.

6.4.2 Proofs

The final task of the author is to check the page proofs. Fortunately, the quality of proofs has generally improved with the use of digital forms of printing, which has largely eliminated the need to retype most of the material. However, there are many opportunities to introduce errors, particularly in mathematical notation. Keep in mind that this is the last chance to correct errors before publication, but do not be tempted to introduce author's changes. These may not be accepted anyway, and can disrupt the carefully prepared page layout, as well as causing further errors to be introduced. However, take the opportunity to revise the bibliography where papers which were initially listed as 'forthcoming' have subsequently appeared in print.

When checking proofs, read the paper several times. First, read it from front to end in the normal way. Then it is helpful to go through it in different directions: moving backwards places the emphasis on each word and avoids the usual problem of allowing the meaning of a sentence to lead to slight errors being missed.

6.5 Conclusions

This chapter has considered the route from manuscript to publication of a journal article. Emphasis was given to the need to deal with rejections and the often substantial revisions requested by editors. While it is suggested that the peer review, or refereeing, process generally provides a useful 'filter' and does lead to improvements being made to papers, it is by no means perfect: for a survey of authors' views, see Leband (1990). Many authors have little difficulty recalling papers which have been made almost incomprehensible by imposed cuts or have had some useful material deleted. There is a substantial element of luck, which means that all journals contain a mixture of qualities. Even those journals with a high average standard have a high dispersion, as well as rejecting papers which, after being published elsewhere, are eventually regarded as making important contributions.

Almost all casual discussions among economists eventually turn to the subject of their recent treatment by journal editors and referees. Colleagues listen with sympathy to terrible stories of injustice, knowing that etiquette requires that their own stories will receive a captive audience. The sympathetic editor and anonymous referees whose constructive suggestions made substantial improvements to a paper, or saved the author from embarrassing errors, are rarely mentioned in such exchanges.

After several years of experience, economists typically have several papers in different stages of the journal submission and production process. They eventually learn how to handle criticism and move on to the next paper or revision, without too much damage being done by a rejection, or too much emphasis being placed on an acceptance. After all, even authors, following a few early shocks, learn to recognise that they are perhaps not always necessarily the best judges of their own papers. And some papers actually turn out to be more valuable than their authors initially thought.

Appendix: An Editor at the Pearly Gates

The editor of an economics journal died, it seemed, from multiple stab wounds in the back. However, there were no witnesses as it was at a conference and most people were in the bar. The editor subsequently appeared in front of St Peter at the pearly gates. The conversation between St Peter and the editor is recorded below.

St Peter: Tell me why you should be admitted to Heaven. What special achievement can you claim?

Economist: My networking finally paid off and I was made editor of an economics journal.

St Peter: That is nothing to boast about.

Economist: But my main claim is that I was the first economics journal editor to remember what it was like to be an author, and I treated all authors as though they were human beings (despite what we actually know about the vast majority of them).

St Peter: Really? Well, this is such an unusual claim that I'll have to consult some of my colleagues about your case. Would you just wait here for a few minutes?

Economist: Yes, I'll just stand here in the shadows.

Two and a half years later the economist was called to appear again in front of St Peter.

St Peter: Sorry for the delay, but I found it very difficult to find colleagues who would talk about your case. They either said they were too busy enjoying themselves, or it wasn't their field. And then the polite reminder note you sent must have blown off my desk ...

Economist: I'm very anxious to know your decision. My future depends on it.

St Peter: My colleagues appear to regard your claim as inconsistent with their models of rational behaviour. They are therefore highly sceptical ...

Economist: But ....

St Peter: ... and no one has ever heard of such a claim, so it can't possibly be true.

Economist: ... but it is, honestly ... I worked hard for years ... making all kinds of sacrifices ... I even apologised to authors when I had to reject their papers!

St Peter: ... and another colleague felt that it is not sufficiently original to warrant entry ...

Economist: But they can't both be right, can they?

St Peter: There appear to be some problems regarding the evidence you cite. Your letters of reference might well be from a highly selective sample ...

Economist: But what is your own view?

St Peter: Well, I think you look like a nice person and your claim is generally well expressed, but of course I'm bound to follow the advice of my colleagues.

Economist: Were there any other problems of which I'm not aware?

St Peter: Importantly, we carried out a survey among representative members of an isolated tribe in the darkest forest of the world, and after translating their responses we found that the journal you edited does not appear in their list of the top five journals. So it must clearly be inferior . . . and doesn't count.

Economist: Do I get another chance to make my claim?

St Peter: Well – I could ask you to go away and revise your case for another couple of years, but on balance I think it would be fair simply to thank you for applying, but . . . *go to* ...!

Bibliography

[1] Allen, R. (1999) *The Pocket New Fowler's Moder English Use*. Oxford: Oxford University Press.

[2] Anderson, J. and Poole, M. (1994) *Thesis and Assignment Writing*. New York: John Wiley and Sons.

[3] Creedy, J. (2001) Starting research. *Australian Economic Review*, 34, pp. 116–124.

[4] Creedy, J. (2006) From manuscript to publication: a brief guide for economists. *Australian Economic Review*, 39, pp. 103–113.

[5] Creedy, J. (2007) A PhD without tears. *Australian Economic Review*, 40, pp. 463-70.

[6] Cutts, M. (1995) *The Plain English Guide*. Oxford: Oxford University Press.

[7] Evans, D. and Gruba, P. (2002) *How to Write a Better Thesis*. Melbourne: Melbourne University Press.

[8] Fischer, C.C. and Lawrence, J.E. (1997) Writing for economics journals: strategic elements. *Journal of Economics*, 23, pp. 31–45.

[9] Gans, J.S. (2000) *Publishing Economics.* Cheltenham: Edward Elgar.

[10] Gans, J.S. and Shephard, G.B. (1994) How are the mighty fallen: rejected classic articles by leading economists. *Journal of Economic Perspectives*, 8, pp. 165–179.

[11] Goffe, W.L. and Parks, R.P. (1997) The future information infrastructure in economics. *Journal of Economic Perspectives*, 11, pp. 75–94.

[12] Hamermesh, D.S. (1992) The young economist's guide to professional etiquette. *Journal of Economic Perspectives*, 6, pp. 169–179.

[13] Hamermesh, D.S. (1994) Facts and myths about refereeing. *Journal of Economic Perspectives*, 8, pp. 153–163.

[14] Huggett, R. (1986) *The Wit of Publishing.* London: W.H. Allen.

[15] Jevons, W.S. (1881) Review of Edgeworth's *Mathematical Psychics. Mind*, 6, pp. 581–583

[16] Law, J. (ed) (2001) *Oxford Language Reference.* Oxford: Oxford University Press.

[17] Leband, D.N. (1990) Is there value-added from the review process in economics?: preliminary evidence from authors. *Quarterly Journal of Economics*, 103, pp. 341–352.

[18] Neugeboren, R.H. (2005) *The Student's Guide to Writing Economics.* New York: Routledge.

[19] Nowell-Smith, S. (1967) *Letters to Macmillan.* London: Macmillan.

[20] Roberts, S.C. (1966) *Adventures With Authors.* Cambridge: Cambridge University Press.

[21] Seely, J. (1998) *The Oxford Guide to Writing and Speaking.* Oxford: Oxford University Press.

[22] Shephard, G. B. (ed.) (1995) *Rejected: Leading Economists Ponder the Publication Process.* Sun Lakes, AZ: Horton.

[23] Taylor, G. (1989) *The Student's Writing Guide for the Arts and Social Sciences.* Cambridge: Cambridge University Press.

[24] Unwin, S. (1926) *The Truth About Publishing.* London: Allen and Unwin.

[25] Unwin, S. (1960) *The Truth About a Publisher.* London: Allen and Unwin.

[26] Viner, J. (1958) *The Long View and The Short.* Glencoe, Illinois: The Free Press.

[27] Weiner, E.S.C. (ed) (1995) *The Oxford Dictionary and English Usage Guide.* Oxford: Oxford University Press.

[28] Wheelock, J.H. (1950) *Editor to Author: The Letters of Maxwell E. Perkins.* New York: Scribners.

Index